A Lenten Companion

Molly Cochran McConnell
Illustrations by March Avery
Photographs by Philip Cavanaugh

MOREHOUSE PUBLISHING
Harrisburg, PA / Wilton, CT

Text and Arrangement copyright © by Molly Cochran McConnell 1990
Illustrations © by March Avery 1990
Photographs © by Philip Cavanaugh 1990

All rights reserved. No part of this book may be reproduced, stored in a retrieval system, or transmitted in any form or by any means, electronic, mechanical, photocopying, recording, or otherwise, without the written permission of the publisher.

Morehouse Publishing

Editorial Office
78 Danbury Road
Wilton, CT 06897

Corporate Office
P.O. Box 1321
Harrisburg, Pa 17105

Library of Congress Cataloging-in-Publication Data
McConnell, Molly.
    A Lenten companion/Molly Cochran McConnell; illustrations by March Avery: photographs by Philip Cavanaugh.
       p. cm.
    ISBN 0-8192-1543-0
    1. Lent—Prayer-books and devotions—English. 2. Devotional calendars—Episcopal Church. 3. Devotional calendars—Catholic Church. 4. Episcopal Church—Prayer-books and devotions—English. 5. Anglican Communion—Prayer-books and devotions—English. 6. Catholic Church—Prayer-books and devotions—English.
I. Title. BV85.M378   1990   90-47610
242'.34—dc20   CIP

Printed in the United States of America
by
BSC Litho
Harrisburg, PA 17105

For Virginia Cochran Noell

Contents

Preface vii

Acknowledgments ix

Introduction xiii

Ash Wednesday and Days Following 1

A Time of Acceptance 9

A Time of Repentance 25

A Time of Obedience 41

A Time of Faithfulness 55

A Time of Thankfulness 69

A Time for Change 85

Easter Is Here 109

Seasonal Recipes 119

Saints' Days During Lent 123

Notes 131

Preface

We all have Lenten periods at various times in our lives. My old, old father's final illness and death coincided with Lent, bringing home anew the Christian meaning of brokenness and healing. We are never too old or too "experienced" to be immune to the shock and pain of death or tragedy in the family. But observing Lent can give form and shape to the path through death and loss to wholeness and healing. Why is it that so many childhood memories come flooding through our minds at the death of a parent? Who can say, but I found the memory of faithfully observing Lent of help in moving through the pain of my father's death. While all of our trials do not always come during Lent, we can observe Lent knowing that the practice of it will help us, fortify us, so that we will not become unmoored and cast about when troubles arrive. For arrive they will.

Lent can be seen as a passage from darkness to light. Observing our natural world come alive from the dormancy of winter, we prepare ourselves spiritually for the triumph of Christ's resurrection at Easter, of the breakthrough of love in our lives by the fulfillment of prophecy and his conquering death.

Death is swallowed up in victory. Death, where is your victory? Death, where is your sting? Now the sting of death is sin, and sin gets its power from the law.
So let us thank God for giving us the victory through our Lord Jesus Christ.
—1 Corinthians 15:55–57

As the weeks rolled by to the other side of Eastertide, almost to Pentecost, I mourned and grieved my father's death. One day I knew healing had occurred.

Death, pain, heartbreak of one kind or another are part

of the fabric of life—my life, your life. Observing Lent at home, alone or with our families, or at church with a study group can begin to "form" us for all the "Lenten moments" in our lives, no matter when they occur.

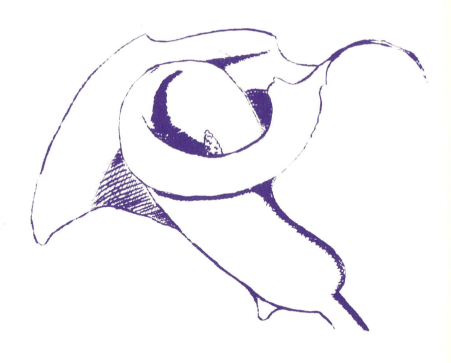

Acknowledgments

Old Testament scripture is from the King James Version of the Holy Bible, 1611.

The author would like to thank the publishers, editors, and authors of the following publications for their kind permission to quote from copyrighted materials:

Excerpts from ABBA by Evelyn Underhill, © 1981 by A.R. Mowbray & Co. Ltd. First USA edition published 1982 by Morehouse-Barlow Co., as part of TREASURES FROM THE SPIRITUAL CLASSICS series.

Excerpts from CHRISTIAN FAITH AND LIFE by William Temple, © 1981 by A.R. Mowbray & Co. Ltd. First USA edition published 1982 by Morehouse-Barlow Co., Inc. as part of TREASURES FROM THE SPIRITUAL CLASSICS series.

Excerpts from FIRST GLANCE AT ADRIENNE von SPEYR by Hans Urs von Balthasar, translated by Antje Lawry and Sr. Sergia Englund O.C.D. © 1981 by Ignatius Press, San Francisco. All rights reserved.

Excerpts from FROM THY BOUNTY by Mary V. Reilly and Margaret K. Wetterer, © 1982 by Mary V. Reilly and Margaret K. Wetterer, published by Morehouse-Barlow Co., Inc. All rights reserved. Recipe for Kulich on p. 120 and recipe for Simnel cake on p. 119.

Excerpts from THE FRUITS OF THE SPIRIT by Evelyn Underhill, © 1981 by A.R. Mowbray & Co. Ltd. First USA edition published 1982 by Morehouse-Barlow Co., Inc. as part of TREASURES FROM THE SPIRITUAL CLASSICS series.

Excerpts from HANDMAID OF THE LORD by Adrienne von Speyr, © 1985 by Ignatius Press, San Francisco. All rights reserved.

Excerpts from THE JERUSALEM BIBLE, © 1966 by Darton, Longman & Todd, Ltd. and Doubleday, a division of Bantam, Doubleday, Dell Publishing Group, Inc. Reprinted by permission.

Excerpts from JESUS AND THE HUNGER FOR THINGS UNKNOWN by Pierre Talec, © 1982 by Seabury Press. Reprinted by permission of Harper & Row, Publishers, Inc.

Excerpts from THE LIFE AND LETTERS OF FATHER ANDREW, SDC by Father Andrew (Henry Ernest Hardy), © 1981 by A.R. Mowbray & Co. Ltd. First USA edition published 1982 by Morehouse-Barlow Co., Inc. as part of TREASURES FROM THE SPIRITUAL CLASSICS series.

Excerpts from LIGHT OF CHRIST by Evelyn Underhill, © 1981 by A.R. Mowbray & Co. Ltd. First USA edition published 1982 by Morehouse-Barlow Co., Inc. as part of TREASURES FROM THE SPIRITUAL CLASSICS series.

Excerpts from THE QUEEN OF PEACE VISITS MEDUGORJE by Joseph A. Pelletier, © 1985, Assumption Publications. All rights reserved.

Excerpts from THE RULE AND EXERCISES OF HOLY LIVING AND THE RULE AND EXERCISES OF HOLY DYING by Jeremy Taylor, © 1981 by A.R. Mowbray & Co. Ltd. First USA edition published 1982 by Morehouse-Barlow Co., Inc. as part of TREASURES FROM THE SPIRITUAL CLASSICS series.

Excerpts from SING THE JOYS OF MARY: *Hymns From the First Millennium of the Eastern and Western Churches*, edited by Costante Berselli and Georges Gharib, translated from the Italian by Phil Jenkins. English translation © 1982 by St. Paul Publications. First USA edition published 1983 by Morehouse-Barlow Co., Inc.

Excerpts from SPIRITUAL LETTERS OF JEAN-PIERRE de CAUSSADE, translated by Kitty Muggeridge, © in the English translation 1986 by William Collins Sons & Co. Ltd., Glasgow. First USA edition published by Morehouse-Barlow Co., Inc.

Excerpts from VERMONT DIARY by Viola White, © 1956, Charles T. Branford, Co. All rights reserved. Permission to quote granted by W. Storrs Lee, literary executor of the estate of Viola White.

Every attempt has been made to credit the sources of copyrighted material used in this book. If any such acknowledgment has been inadvertently omitted or miscredited, receipt of such information would be appreciated.

Introduction

Lent is a season of penitence and fasting during the six-and-a-half-week period preceding Easter. Breaking into the rhythm of fasting and penitence are six Sundays on which we celebrate the resurrection glory of our risen Lord. Moses, Elijah, and our Lord each made forty-day fasts, thus the tradition today of forty days of fasting preceding Easter.

During the early centuries of the Church, fasts were strictly observed and allowed only one meal a day, taken toward evening. Meat, fish, eggs, and milk products were absolutely forbidden. Through the centuries these practices were gradually relaxed.

Liturgically, this season is marked by the wearing of purple vestments and the omission of the *Alleluia* and (excepting great feasts) the *Gloria in excelsis* during the eucharist. There is, however, a relaxation of the rules of Lent on the fourth Sunday (see the section in this chapter, "Laetare Sunday").

Lent, a time of repentance, is observed by prayer, fasting, and self-denial. Reading and meditating on God's Word and almsgiving also characterize the period.

Since Easter is a movable feast, Lent can begin from any time in early February to mid-March, depending upon the year.

SHROVE TUESDAY

No discussion of Lent is complete without mentioning Shrove Tuesday, although it precedes Lent, falling on the day before Ash Wednesday. Shrovetide, three days preceding the beginning of Lent, and Shrove Tuesday in particular, is a time of revelry before the time of denial ushered in by Lent. The name comes from the English custom of going to church for shriving, which is confession of one's sins and absolution, before the start of Lent.

Carnival—Fasching from the German; Mardi Gras (Fat Tuesday) from the French—has roots other than Christian ones. It is similar in many ways to the Jewish feast of Purim celebrating the deliverance of the Jews from the Persians brought about by Queen Esther (see chapter 9 of the Old Testament Book of Esther).

There are also pagan origins of Carnival. In parts of Germany, there were pagan rites of driving out winter and banishing demonic power. Certainly, we all are familiar with merrymaking on the streets of New Orleans during Mardi Gras. Wherever Carnival is celebrated in the Christian world, it marks a "letting go" and celebration before the seriousness and "putting on" of penitential acts of Lent.

Not surprisingly, food is connected with the occasion. Folk wisdom says that, historically, foods were used up—the equivalant of a present day "fridge cleaning"—the day before the beginning of Lent.

ASH WEDNESDAY

Ash Wednesday, the first day of Lent, is a fast day in both the Anglican and Roman Catholic traditions. Ashes, made from burning palms from Palm Sunday of the preceding year, are imposed on the foreheads of both clergy and people in memory of their mortality and penitence, "Remember that you are dust, and to dust you shall return."

ASH WEDNESDAY AND DAYS FOLLOWING

READING FOR ASH WEDNESDAY

Bless the Lord, O my soul: and all that is within
me, bless his holy name.
Bless the Lord, O my soul, and forget not all his
benefits:
who forgiveth all thine iniquities; who healeth all
thy diseases;
who redeemeth thy life from destruction; who
crowneth thee with loving-kindness and tender
mercies;
who satisfieth thy mouth with good things;
so that thy youth is renewed like the eagle's.

The Lord executeth righteousness and judgment for
all that are oppressed.
He made known his ways unto Moses, his acts unto
the children of Israel.
The Lord is merciful and gracious, slow to anger,
and plenteous in mercy.
He will not always chide: neither will he keep his
anger for ever.

He hath not dealt with us after our sins; nor rewarded
us according to our iniquities.
For as the heaven is high above the earth, so great
is his mercy toward them that fear him.
As far as the east is from the west, so far hath he
removed our transgressions from us.
Like as a father pitieth his children, so the Lord
pitieth them that fear him.
For he knoweth our frame; he remembereth that
we are dust.

As for man, his days are as grass: as a flower of the
field, so he flourisheth.
For the wind passeth over it, and it is gone; and the
place thereof shall know it no more,
But the mercy of the Lord is from everlasting to
everlasting upon them that fear him, and his
righteousness unto children's children;

*to such as keep his covenant, and to those that
remember his commandments to do them.
The Lord hath prepared his throne in the heavens;
and his kingdom ruleth over all.
Bless the Lord, ye his angels, that excel in strength,
that do his commandments, hearkening unto the
voice of his word.
Bless ye the Lord, all ye his hosts; ye ministers of
his, that do his pleasure.
Bless the Lord, all his works in all places of his
dominion: bless the Lord, O my soul.*
—*Psalm 103*

Dear Lord, let us remember this Ash Wednesday that all life comes from you and heads toward you. Be near as we travel the Way.

READINGS FOR THURSDAY
LENT IS A TIME FOR PRAYER.

> *Give ear to my words, O Lord; consider my meditation.*
> *Hearken unto the voice of my cry, my King, and my God: for unto thee will I pray.*
> *My voice shalt thou hear in the morning, O Lord; in the morning will I direct my prayer unto thee, and will look up.*
>
> —Psalm 5:1–3

> *And I set my face unto the Lord God, to seek by prayer and supplications, with fasting, and sackcloth, and ashes: and I prayed unto the Lord my God, and made my confession, and said, O Lord, the great and dreadful God, keeping the covenant and mercy to them that love him, and to them that keep his commandments; we have sinned, and have committed iniquity, and have done wickedly, and have rebelled, even by departing from thy precepts and from thy judgments: neither have we hearkened unto thy servants the prophets, which spake in thy name to our kings, our princes, and our fathers, and to all the people of the land. . . .*
>
> *O Lord, hear; O Lord, forgive; O Lord, hearken and do; defer not, for thine own sake, O my God: for thy city and thy people are called by thy name.*
>
> —Daniel 9:3–6, 19

Help us to open our hearts in prayer, good Lord.

READING FOR FRIDAY
LENT IS A TIME FOR FASTING.

> "When you fast do not put on a gloomy look as the hypocrites do: they pull long faces to let men know they are fasting. I tell you solemnly, they have had their reward. But when you fast, put oil on your head and wash your face, so that no one will know you are fasting except your Father who sees all that is done in secret; and your Father who sees all that is done in secret will reward you."
>
> —Matthew 6:16–18

Lord, help us to commit ourselves to fasting and in so doing come closer to you.

READING FOR SATURDAY
LENT IS A TIME FOR ALMSGIVING.

> "For I was hungry and you gave me food; I was thirsty and you gave me drink; I was a stranger and you made me welcome; naked and you clothed me, sick and you visited me, in prison and you came to see me." Then the virtuous will say to him in reply, "Lord, when did we see you hungry and feed you; or thirsty and give you drink? When did we see you a stranger and make you welcome; naked and clothe you; sick or in prison and go to see you?" And the King will answer, "I tell you solemnly, in so far as you did this to one of the least of these brothers of mine, you did it to me."
> —Matthew 25:35–40

Dear Lord, help us to see the needs of others and to work to relieve them as best we can throughout this Lenten period.

A Time of Acceptance
The First Week of Lent

ACCEPTANCE

Lent is a time of acceptance: of ourselves, our needs, and our paths of error; of others and our obligations to them. Observing the traditional three areas of focus in Lent—prayer, fasting, and almsgiving—we can draw closer to our Lord and come to understand better his will for us. By the discipline of fasting and self-denial we are reminded of all that our Lord did for us. By almsgiving we can reach out to others in a special way during Lent.

In spite of the fact we are all too busy most of the time, we can always find an extra few minutes to pray—while waiting in traffic, riding the bus to work, or even standing in line. One friend of mine even keeps a book of meditations in the glove compartment of her car.

Observing any kind of fast focuses our attention on habitual patterns of action and turns it from them to the "why" of our fast. Our Lord suffered and gave up his life for us—let us not forget this. The heightened attention that we gain by fasting can enable us to make changes in our lives. Perhaps it is time to think about our bodies and whether or not we are being good stewards of them. I grew up in a household where meatless days were observed on Ash Wednesday and Fridays in Lent—fish days they were. Try changing your accustomed routine during Lent.

Giving up something can enable us to give in other ways. Perhaps we can use the money saved to give toward filling a need that we know of in the community. Or we can keep a Lenten coin box and take it to church when the fasting days of Lent are over.

Consider accepting a different daily routine during Lent. It can make a difference in both your understanding and celebration of the joy of Easter.

THE GLORY OF THESE FORTY DAYS

*The glory of these forty days
We celebrate with songs of praise;
For Christ, by whom all things were made,
Himself has fasted and has prayed.*

*Alone and fasting Moses saw
The loving God who gave the law;
And to Elijah, fasting, came
The steeds and chariots of flame.*

*So Daniel trained his mystic sight,
Delivered from the lions' might;
And John, the Bridegroom's friend, became
The herald of Messiah's name.*

*Then grant us, Lord, like them to be
Full oft in fast and prayer with thee;
Our spirits strengthen with thy grace,
And give us joy to see thy face.*

*O Father, Son, and Spirit blest,
To thee be every prayer addrest,
Who art in threefold Name adored,
From age to age, the only Lord.*

—Latin, ca. sixth century

READING FOR SUNDAY

You were darkness once, but now you are light in the Lord; be like children of light, for the effects of the light are seen in complete goodness and right living and truth. Try to discover what the Lord wants of you, having nothing to do with the futile works of darkness but exposing them by contrast.

—*Ephesians 5:8–11*

Lord, grant that with your help we may move from the darkness in our lives to the light.

READINGS FOR MONDAY

A day of blinding silver light and extreme cold. All the trees above and below the falls are frosted. . . .
—Viola White

Jesus is he who by his death and Resurrection established the passage from darkness to light.
—Pierre Talec

Blessed be the Lord, the God of Israel,
for he has visited his people, and he has come
to their rescue
and he has raised up for us a power for salvation
in the House of his servant David,
even as he proclaimed,
by the mouth of his holy prophets from
ancient times,
that he would save us from our enemies
and from the hands of all who hate us.
Thus he shows mercy to our ancestors,
thus he remembers his holy covenant,
the oath he swore
to our father Abraham

*that he would grant us, free from fear,
to be delivered from the hands of our enemies,
to serve him in holiness and virtue
in his presence,
all our days.
And you, little child,
you shall be called Prophet of the Most High,
for you will go before the Lord
to prepare the way for him.
To give his people knowledge of salvation
through the forgiveness of their sins;
this by the tender mercy of our God
who from on high will bring the rising Sun
to visit us,
to give light to those who live
in darkness and the shadow of death,
and to guide our feet
into the way of peace.*
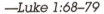
—Luke 1:68–79

Dear Lord, for those in darkness give thy light and peace this day.

READINGS FOR TUESDAY

A little blizzard started in the later afternoon, and we are back in the depths of winter once more.
—*Viola White*

There is only one cure for fear; that is just trust in the love of God. The great honor that God paid to our Blessed Lady was just His trust in her trust of Him. So He could ask her to accept St. Joseph's doubt, the sight of the Beloved crucified. "Be it unto me according to Thy word," said the girl of Nazareth, and we must say it, too, and trust that *word* whatever it may hold in it of earthly experience, for His Word has been written in letters of joy and pain, and weariness and blood, but the Finger that has been dipped in the different colors of life's fluid stream has always been the Finger of Love.
—*Father Andrew*

"I am the handmaid of the Lord," said Mary, "let what you have said be done to me...."
And Mary said:

*"My soul proclaims the greatness of the Lord
and my spirit exults in God my savior;
because he has looked upon his lowly handmaid.
Yes, from this day forward all generations will
call me blessed,
for the Almighty has done great things for me.
Holy is his name,
and his mercy reaches from age to age
for those who fear him.
He has shown the power of his arm,
he has routed the proud of heart.
He has pulled down princes from their thrones
and exalted the lowly.
The hungry he has filled with good things, the
rich sent empty away.
He has come to the help of Israel his servant,
mindful of his mercy
—according to the promise he made to our
ancestors—
of his mercy to Abraham and to his descendants
for ever."*

—Luke 1:38, 46–58

Lord, grant us the peace of mind and calmness to understand our part in your plan. And understanding it, let us act on it.

READINGS FOR WEDNESDAY

Out in the deep wet snow with the dogs this morning. It's always foolish to take them out in this kind of snow for they became encrusted with it and soon resemble snowballs. A woodpecker's rat-a-tat is echoing up the mountain. *I wonder where it is.*

Do not try to alter circumstances. Follow the example of Kituzou in *War and Peace*. He overcame Napoleon by *waiting* and doing *nothing* except what it was obvious to do at the moment. God will bring about His will out of circumstances if we leave it to Him and live in union with Him.

—*Father Andrew*

In your prayers do not babble as the pagans do, for they think that by using many words they will make themselves heard. Do not be like them; your father knows what you need before you ask him. So you should pray like this:

*Our Father in heaven,
may your name be held holy,
your kingdom come,
your will be done,
on earth as in heaven.
Give us today our daily bread.
And forgive us our debts,
as we forgive those who are in debt to us.
And do not put us to the test,
but save us from the evil one."*

—Matthew 6:7–13

Grant me the patience to listen to you, Lord Christ.

READINGS FOR THURSDAY

Raw and quite windy. The Adirondacks are frosted with more fresh snow. I can hear the sound of the snow shovel hitting the driveway. Its rhythm provides a background for the birds' flyway across the side yard from the feeder to the brush thicket at the edge of the lawn.

... a situation, contrast, test, demand, always turning up in the devout life—that call of those who need taking us away from what we love to do. Do we meet it with exasperation or unwillingness, or with the power of a great compassion, united to the love of God? We are each one of us an instrument of His rescuing action; our lives as Christians are not complete without that, and His power will not be exerted through us except at considerable cost to ourselves. How gentle, humble, uncritical, full of zest we have got to be, if that power is to have a free path!
—*Evelyn Underhill*

When Jesus spoke to the people again, he said: "I am the light of the world; anyone who follows me will not be walking in the dark; he will have the light of life."
—*John 8:12*

Lord, help us to hear your call and, upon hearing it, follow.

READINGS FOR FRIDAY

Took the dogs for a walk along the ice encrusted snow. About a mile from the house along the closed end of our road is a wonder of nature—a pile of wood chips perhaps two feet tall from a woodpecker's recent work. The dead tree, tall and noble with its markings, bears testimony to the survival of some of nature during this bitterly cold winter.

Calm, O maiden most pure,
the wild storm of my soul,
for you alone showed yourself on earth to be
the port of all who set a course
through the perils of life.
—Joseph the Studite

In view of the extraordinary nature of these revelations, to stop me from getting too proud I was given a thorn in the flesh, an angel of Satan to beat me and stop me from getting too proud! About this thing, I have pleaded with the Lord three times for it to leave me, but he has said, "My grace is enough for you: my power is at its best in weakness." So I

shall be very happy to make my weaknesses my special boast so that the power of Christ may stay over me, and that is why I am quite content with my weaknesses, and with insults, hardships, persecutions, and the agonies I go through for Christ's sake. For it is when I am weak that I am strong.
—*2 Corinthians 12:7–10*

May we learn patience to accept gracefully those troublesome parts of our lives, knowing that through your grace there can be strength in weakness.

READINGS FOR SATURDAY

Warmer and sunny, just above freezing, funny what gives us hope of spring in these northern climes. The sun *is* warmer today. We've had such extremes of weather lately that it's a wonder we aren't sick.

The odd thing is that our ordinary, everyday life experiences can sometimes open spiritual doors that esoteric ascetic practices may fail to open. Sometimes these experiences may on the surface be painful or even cruel—but they have been known to bring people face to face with the Holy Spirit. Sometimes fate steps in and confronts people with illness, or deformity, the loss of a spouse, sterility, forced celibacy. All these can be seen as a terrible blow to endure or disabilities to overcome. But they can also bring about a release, a new life.
—*Pierre Talec*

Come to me, all you who labor and are overburdened, and I will give you rest. Shoulder my yoke and learn from me, for I am gentle and

humble in heart, and you will find rest for your souls. Yes, my yoke is easy and my burden light.
—*Matthew 11:28–30*

Lord, help me to turn to you when I feel overwhelmed and grant that I may find rest and peace by accepting my burdens and following you.

A TIME OF REPENTANCE
The Second Week of Lent

REPENTANCE

Lent is a time of repentance. Conflict within because of those things we've done which we should not have done, plus regret for those things left undone, are part of our human condition. We all have these troubling feelings. Lent is a time for remembering these things and for offering them to God in prayer. Then, we must let go of them.

Many Christians attend confession regularly. Others ask for special services of penance. Some find release by writing daily in a journal or in private meditations. Any one of these can help us to let go.

Let a goal for this second week in Lent be repentance and acceptance of our own cross. We can try to pick up and to carry gracefully the cross our Lord has given to each one of us. Carrying our cross—our personal burden, that which we would really rather someone else carry—implies acceptance, self-denial, and forgiveness. With God's help we can accept our crosses and live with them. "Things that are impossible for men," Jesus said, "are possible for God." (Luke 18:27).

WILT THOU FORGIVE?

Wilt thou forgive that sin, where I begun,
which is my sin, though it were done before?
Wilt thou forgive those sins through which I run,
and do run still, though still I do deplore?
When thou hast done, thou hast not done, for I have more.

Wilt thou forgive that sin, by which I won
others to sin, and made my sin their door?
Wilt thou forgive that sin which I did shun
a year or two, but wallowed in a score?
When thou hast done, thou hast not done, for I have more.

I have a sin of fear that when I've spun
my last thread, I shall perish on the shore;
swear by thyself, that at my death thy Son
shall shine as he shines now, and here-to-fore.
And having done that, thou hast done, I fear no more.

—John Donne
1573–1631

READING FOR SUNDAY

He that dwelleth in the secret place of the Most High
shall abide under the shadow of the Almighty.
I will say of the Lord, He is my refuge and my
fortress: my God; in him will I trust.
Surely he shall deliver thee from the snare of the
fowler, and from the noisome pestilence.
He shall cover thee with his feathers, and under his
wings shalt thou trust: his truth shall be thy shield
and buckler.
Thou shalt not be afraid for the terror by night; nor
for the arrow that flieth by day;
nor for the pestilence that walketh in darkness; nor
for the destruction that wasteth at noonday.
A thousand shall fall at thy side, and ten thousand
at thy right hand; but it shall not come nigh thee.
Only with thine eyes shalt thou behold and see the
reward of the wicked.
Because thou hast made the Lord, which is my refuge,
even the Most High, thy habitation;
there shall no evil befall thee, neither shall any
plague come nigh thy dwelling.
For he shall give his angels charge over thee, to
keep thee in all thy ways.
They shall bear thee up in their hands, lest thou dash
thy foot against a stone.
Thou shalt tread upon the lion and adder: the young
lion and the dragon shalt thou trample under feet.
Because he hath set his love upon me, therefore will
I deliver him: I will set him on high, because he
hath known my name.
He shall call upon me, and I will answer him: I will
be with him in trouble; I will deliver him and honor
him,
With long life will I satisfy him, and show him my
salvation.

—Psalm 91

Hear me, good Lord, when I am troubled and call.

READINGS FOR MONDAY

Northern winters are so long and harsh; the need to get out and be renewed is crucial. Some days a brisk walk is quite refreshing—if nothing else it makes me glad to  return to the warmth of the house. My favorite walk is a twenty-minute one around our hilly hayfield. The tracks in the snow are fascinating. There is a huge rabbit who lives nearby and at least three deer who make comfortable-looking nests for themselves in our hayfield. Their tracks criss-crossing the nests lead me to think that they perform a nightly dance before retiring.

We are living in a time of grace during which God is calling us to repent and turn back to him.

—*Joseph A. Pelletier*

Ho, every one that thirsteth, come ye to the waters, and he that hath no money; come ye, buy, and eat; yea, come, buy wine and milk without money and without price. . . . Seek ye the Lord while he may be

found, call ye upon him while he is near: let the wicked forsake his way, and the unrighteous man his thoughts: and let him return unto the Lord, and he will have mercy upon him; and to our God, for he will abundantly pardon.

—Isaiah 55:1, 6–7

We turn to you for forgiveness and mercy, dear Lord.

READINGS FOR TUESDAY

A bit warmer today. It rained in the night, and the roads are icy. No newspaper until after the cinder spreader came. What a welcome sound that heavy plow is as it lumbers up the road to our place.

Since Jesus Christ crucified is our only example, and since He wishes to save us by letting us be like Him, He sows crosses in the path to salvation for each one of us. If we are faithful, these frustrations that cross our path will enrich us.
—Jean-Pierre de Caussade

Then Jesus said to his disciples, "If anyone wants to be a follower of mine, let him renounce himself and take up his cross and follow me."
—Matthew 16:24

Help us to see and accept the cross that is part of the fabric of everyday life, good Lord.

READINGS FOR WEDNESDAY

A fog seems to have settled upon us. It is cold and gray with a promise of rain or snow. Snow would be preferable as there is still icy slush on the road. I wish I could store up this wetness for a hot summer's day. Perhaps the water table will rise. Our well's pump is over two hundred feet below the ground. How glad I am that we had the pipes relaid last summer. Frozen pipes are nothing to laugh about.

. . . fasting liberates the mind and spirit, disposing us to pray.
—Joseph A. Pelletier

And the word of the Lord came unto Jonah the second time, saying, Arise, go unto Nineveh, that great city, and preach unto it the preaching that I bid thee. So Jonah arose, and went unto Nineveh, according to the word of the Lord. Now Nineveh was an exceeding great city of three days' journey. And Jonah began to enter into the city a day's journey, and he cried, and said, Yet forty days, and Nineveh

shall be overthrown. So the people of Nineveh believed God, and proclaimed a fast, and put on sackcloth, from the greatest of them even to the least of them.

For word came unto the king of Nineveh, and he arose from his throne, and he laid his robe from him, and covered him with a sackcloth, and sat in ashes. And he caused it to be proclaimed and published through Nineveh by the decree of the king and his nobles, saying, Let neither man nor beast, herd nor flock, taste any thing: let them not feed, nor drink water: but let man and beast be covered with sackcloth, and cry mightily unto God: yea, let them turn every one from his evil way, and from the violence that is in their hands. Who can tell if God will turn and repent, and turn away from his fierce anger, that we perish not?

And God saw their works, that they turned from their evil way; and God repented of the evil, that he had said that he would do unto them; and he did it not.

—Jonah 3

Lord, let us repent and turn from our ways of wrongdoing. Be merciful to us.

READINGS FOR THURSDAY

Light flurries and cold. Sun may break through. Newspapers say that we all suffer depression from days without sunlight. I try to turn on as many lights as possible during this time of late winter. My desk looks out of a large, well-insulated window. I seem to need much light.

What have I begun, and what accomplished?
To what did I reach out, for what do I long?
I sought after goodness, and lo, here is turmoil;
I was going towards God, and I was my own
impediment. I sought for peace within myself,
And in the depths of my heart I found trouble and
sorrow. I wanted to laugh for the joy of my heart,
And the pain of my heart made me groan.
It was gladness I was hoping for,
but sighs came thick and fast.
—*Saint Anselm*

Be at peace among yourselves. And this is what we ask you to do, brothers: warn the idlers, give courage to those who are apprehensive, care for the weak and be patient with everyone. Make sure that

people do not try to take revenge; you must all think of what is best for each other and for the community. Be happy at all times; pray constantly; and for all things give thanks to God, because this is what God expects you to do in Christ Jesus.

Never try to suppress the Spirit or treat the gift of prophecy with contempt; think before you do anything—hold on to what is good and avoid every form of evil.

—*1 Thessalonians 5:14–22*

Help us, good Lord, to live according to your Word.

READINGS FOR FRIDAY

Cold and snowing hard. In spite of all the trouble snow creates, I must confess that I love its quiet beauty. Suddenly, the barren brown fields are covered with a white blanket; curving dark limbs highlighted by an accent that looks like an artist's stroke.

Repentance does not merely mean giving up a bad habit. What it is concerned with is the mind; get a new mind. What mind? The mind of Christ—our standard of reference; learn to look at the world in His way. To repent is to adopt God's viewpoint in place of your own. There need not be any sorrow about it. In itself, far from being sorrowful, it is the most joyful thing in the world, because when you have done it you have adopted the viewpoint of truth itself, and you are in fellowship with God. It means a complete re-valuation of all things we are inclined to think good. The world, as we live in it, is like a shop window in which some mischievous person has got over-night and shifted all the price-labels round so that the cheap things have the high price-labels on them, and the really precious things are priced low. We let ourselves be taken in. Repentance means getting those price-labels back in the right place.

—William Temple

Then to all he said, "If anyone wants to be a follower of mine, let him renounce himself and take up his cross every day and follow me. For anyone who wants to save his life will lose it; but anyone who loses his life for my sake, that man will save it."
—Luke 9:23–24

Help us to live a life deeply rooted in you, Lord Christ.

READINGS FOR SATURDAY

Bitterly cold and sunny—well below zero. The sun, lacking warmth, does sparkle on the snow, creating a diamondlike effect. It's so cold that the dogs and I can walk across the top of the snow. But what house-dweller can stay out long in this?

Not what we give, but what we share—
For the gift without the giver is bare;
Who gives himself with his alms feeds three—
    Himself, his hungering neighbor, and me.
                                —James Russell Lowell

Be careful not to parade your good deeds before men to attract their notice; by doing this you will lose all reward from your Father in heaven. So when you give alms, do not have it trumpeted before you; this is what the hypocrites do in the synagogues and in the streets to win men's admiration. I tell you solemnly, they have had their reward. But when you give alms, your left hand must not know what your right is doing; your almsgiving must be secret, and

your Father who sees all that is done in secret will reward you.

—*Matthew 6:1–4*

Through fasting and prayer this Lent, help us to see the needs of others and to give graciously to relieve them.

A TIME OF OBEDIENCE

The Third Week of Lent

OBEDIENCE

Lent is a time of obedience. We don't hear much these days about the place of obedience in our lives. And yet every one of us has a need for obedience, for faithfulness. Our Lord learned obedience through what he suffered. We, too, can learn obedience through our sufferings.

By practicing obedience to our Lord, we can also learn patience and trust. Committing our lives to him, we are enabled to carry our cross. What is our cross? My cross? Your cross? Each one is different. Mine is not the same as yours. Different though our crosses may be, our needs are similar.

During this third week of Lent, let us try to be obedient to the regimen or routine we've chosen to follow this year. Perhaps we have given up things that will free us for activities in other areas. Perhaps an attitude like impatience or habit like overworking can be mastered in such a way that we will be free for other things, such as spending more time and care with our families or working to help the needy, the homeless, or those who suffer from illness.

Obedience to Jesus means following him. Let us practice that especially this third week of Lent.

KIND MAKER OF THE WORLD, O HEAR

Kind Maker of the world, O hear
The fervent prayer, with many a tear
Poured forth by all the penitent
Who keep this holy fast of Lent!

Each heart is manifest to thee;
Thou knowest our infirmity;
Now we repent, and seek thy face;
Grant unto us thy pardoning grace.

Spare us, O Lord, who now confess
Our sins and all our wickedness,
And, for the glory of thy Name,
Our weakened souls to health reclaim.

Give us the self-control that springs
From abstinence in outward things;
That from each stain and spot of sin,
Our souls may keep the fast within.

Grant, O thou blesséd Trinity;
Grant, O unchanging Unity;
That this our fast of forty days
May work our profit and thy praise!

—Saint Gregory the Great
ca. 540–604

READING FOR SUNDAY

I will bless the Lord at all times: his praise shall
  continually be in my mouth.
My soul shall make her boast in the Lord: the humble
  shall hear thereof, and be glad.
O magnify the Lord with me, and let us exalt his
  name together.

I sought the Lord, and he heard me, and delivered
  me from all my fears.
They looked unto him, and were lightened: and
  their faces were not ashamed.
This poor man cried, and the Lord heard him, and
  saved him out of all his troubles.

The angel of the Lord encampeth round about them
  that fear him, and delivereth them.
O taste and see that the Lord is good: blessed is the
  man that trusteth in him.
O fear the Lord, ye his saints: for there is no want to
  them that fear him.
The young lions do lack, and suffer hunger: but
  they that seek the Lord shall not want any good
  thing.

Come, ye children, hearken unto me: I will teach
  you the fear of the Lord.
What man is he that desireth life, and loveth many
  days, that he may see good?
Keep thy tongue from evil, and thy lips from
  speaking guile.
Depart from evil, and do good; seek peace, and
  pursue it.

The eyes of the Lord are upon the righteous, and
  his ears are open unto their cry.
The face of the Lord is against them that do evil,
  to cut off the remembrance of them from the
  earth.

*The righteous cry, and the Lord heareth, and
   delivereth them out of all their troubles.
The Lord is nigh unto them that are of a broken
   heart; and saveth such as be of a contrite spirit.*

*Many are the afflictions of the righteous: but the
   Lord delivereth him out of them all.
He keepeth all his bones: not one of them is broken.
Evil shall slay the wicked: and they that hate the
   righteous shall be desolate.
The Lord redeemeth the soul of his servants: and
   none of them that trust in him shall be desolate.*
—Psalm 34

Strengthen my trust in you, Lord Christ. Be with me when I call.

READINGS FOR MONDAY

Extremely cold, sunny; ice on the brook. The days are decidedly longer. A bit more light at the beginning of the day, a longer day-lit afternoon.

In your work submit to God, but without bustle or impatience. Just do your best at what you think is your duty and then leave all the rest to Providence, without a care or anxiety, so as to have as far as possible a free spirit and a quiet heart. You will remain at peace in the midst of difficulties and confusion by conforming to the merciful and indulgent will of God.
—Jean-Pierre de Caussade

But he has been even more generous to us, as scripture says: God opposes the proud but he gives generously to the humble. Give in to God, then; resist the devil, and he will run away from you. The nearer you go to God, the nearer he will come to you. . . . Humble yourselves before the Lord and he will lift you up.
—James 4:6–8, 10

Dear Lord, help us to learn patience and humility so that our lives will reflect them.

READINGS FOR TUESDAY

First morning we awoke to daylight—the lengthening days give hints of spring.

As a sheaf of grain is tied together in the middle and spreads out at either end, so Mary's life is bound together by her assent. . . . This is the nature of an assent: it binds the one who gives it, yet it allows him complete freedom in shaping its expression. He fills his assent with his personality, giving it its weight and unique coloring. But he himself is also molded, liberated and fulfilled by his assent. All freedom develops through surrender and through renunciation of liberty. And from this freedom within commitment there arises every sort of fruitfulness.
—*Adrienne von Speyr*

The sheep that belong to me listen to my voice;
I know them and they follow me.
I give them eternal life;
they will never be lost
and no one will ever steal them from me.
—*John 10:27–28*

Teach us to listen so that we may hear and understand you and each other, Lord Christ.

READINGS FOR WEDNESDAY

Cold, sunny; hints of spring are in the air: the bird sounds are changing. Could it be that some birds are returning? Or perhaps the winter residents are only responding to more daylight. We've chickadees, cardinals, blue jays, nuthatches, and finches that frequent our feeder in a maple tree in the front yard. Ted has willingly committed himself to feeding them early each morning.

"Leave everything!" But the Gospel is really not all or nothing. In the *all of life*, Christ suggests little *nothings* to us. Christ knows how to view those nothings as an all when they express the all of life dedicated to him. He doesn't ask more of us than he has empowered us to give.

—*Pierre Talec*

He was in the world
that had its being through him,
and the world did not know him.
He came to his own domain
and his own people did not accept him.
But to all who did accept him

*he gave power to become the children of God,
to all who believe in the name of him who was born
not out of human stock
or urge of the flesh
or will of man
but of God himself.*

—John 1:10–13

Increase our faith, dear Lord. Help us to understand more clearly what following you means.

READINGS FOR THURSDAY

Today is bone-chilling cold but rainy; at least there is no snow. Perhaps the rain will clean off things.

Healing love must drop all personal choices and preferences, all fastidiousness, all desire to get something out of our union with Christ; and be willing to work for nothing, be a faithful servant, not a pet. We may have to see all the resources of Divine Love poured out on a damaged and undeserving Prodigal, the fatted calf, the music and dancing— while we are left in the unemotional and hardworking position of the elder son. Only perfect self-oblivion is going to handle that situation well. "Son, thou art ever with me and all that I have is thine. But only if you use it as I use it; come in with me as a partner, pour it out without stint in spendthrift generosity on those who need restoration and healing, not those who deserve it."

If our call to share the life of Christ the Teacher lays the Cross upon the intellect, our call to share the life of Christ the Healer lays the Cross upon the heart.
—Evelyn Underhill

Although he was Son, he learned to obey through suffering; but having been made perfect, he became for all who obey him the source of eternal salvation and was acclaimed by God with the title of high priest of the order of Melchizedek.
—Hebrews 5:8–10

May we know through obedience to you that inner peace that only you can give.

READINGS FOR FRIDAY

Beautiful, clear, sunny, cold day—gorgeous sunrise—fireball through the foggy mist hovering over the river. The vast morning sky is spectacular.

Her obedience is the prototype of every future instance of Christian obedience, which draws its whole meaning from the life of prayer and the perception of God's will. For Mary, however, God's will in its certainty has not yet become apparent. She is still waiting for the declaration of this will. She is ready in prayer to accept it even when she does not know what she will be accepting. She knows perfect indifference; and whoever among the generations of future Christians knows about the meaning and the extent of indifference will owe this knowledge most of all to the Mother.
—*Adrienne von Speyr*

He called the people and his disciples to him and said, "If anyone wants to be a follower of mine, let him renounce himself and take up his cross and follow me."
—*Mark 8:34*

Help us to understand and to grow in obedience to you, Lord Christ.

READINGS FOR SATURDAY

Cold and sunny; hints of spring abound. Pruned roses and cut a bit of forsythia and quince to force in bloom in the house. There's much cutting and raking to do. I feel a sense of urgency and rising energy to get ready for the growing season.

Finally, speak to him of the need to cherish that most precious spiritual treasure which is inner calm and peace of the soul, that comes from obeying the bountiful and holy will of God in confidence and submission to His fatherly Providence united in Jesus Christ, to His example and the example of those who become saints by conforming to it.
—Jean-Pierre de Caussade

God is our refuge and strength, a very present help in trouble.
Therefore will not we fear, though the earth be removed, and though the mountains be carried into the midst of the sea;
though the waters thereof roar and be troubled, though the mountains shake with the swelling thereof. . . .

> There is a river, the streams whereof shall make
> glad the city of God, the holy place of the
> tabernacles of the Most High.
> God is in the midst of her; she shall not be moved:
> God shall help her, and that right early.
> The heathen raged, the kingdoms were moved: he
> uttered his voice, the earth melted.
> The Lord of hosts is with us; the God of Jacob
> is our refuge. . . .
>
> Come, behold the works of the Lord, what desola-
> tions he hath made in the earth.
> He maketh wars to cease unto the end of the earth;
> he breaketh the bow, and cutteth the spear in
> sunder;
> he burneth the chariot in the fire.
> Be still, and know that I am God: I will be exalted
> among the heathen, I will be exalted in the earth.
> The Lord of hosts is with us; the God of Jacob
> is our refuge. . . .
>
> —Psalm 46

Lord, help us to find stillness and quiet in our busy lives so that we may know you.

A TIME OF FAITHFULNESS
The Fourth Week of Lent

FAITHFULNESS

Lent is a time of faithfulness. A time during which we can try to understand better God's will for us and, understanding it, be faithful to it. Through prayer and meditation, we can work on becoming more patient, more humble, more open to direction from our Lord.

Being faithful to God means being fully ourselves and means loving our neighbor. It means giving attention to the small, insignificant things in life. Taking time for the half-hidden, seemingly unimportant is not easy. But it is a part of the meaning of following Christ. Let us grow in faithfulness this Lent.

LAETARE SUNDAY

The fourth Sunday in Lent, mi-carême from the French, marks the midpoint in Lent. This day is often known as Mothering Sunday or Refreshment Sunday and is a time when Lenten rules are relaxed. The day is often celebrated by the wearing of rose-pink vestments and by serving simnel cake after the Eucharist. In parts of England it is customary to visit one's mother on this day. There is also the custom of visiting the "mother church" or cathedral on Laetare Sunday in England. The traditional Scripture reading for this day ("But Jerusalem which is above is free, which is the mother of us all," Gal. 4:26, KJV) may be the source of the name Mothering Sunday. Or some say that children in England, apprenticed out away from home, were permitted to return home on that day. They took simnel cake to sustain them during the journey (for recipe, see page 119).

FROM DEEPEST WOE I CRY TO THEE

From deepest woe I cry to thee; Lord, hear me, I implore thee!
Bend down thy gracious ear to me; I lay my sins before thee.
If thou rememberest every sin, if nought but just reward we win,
could we abide thy presence?

Thou grantest pardon through thy love; thy grace alone
 availeth.
Our works could ne'er our guilt remove; yea, e'en the best life
 faileth.
For none may boast themselves of aught, but must confess thy
 grace hath wrought
whate'er in them is worthy.

And thus my hope is in the Lord, and not in my own merit;
I rest upon his faithful word to them of contrite spirit.
That he is merciful and just, here is my comfort and my trust;
his help I wait with patience.

—Martin Luther
1483–1546

READING FOR SUNDAY

Rejoice ye with Jerusalem, and be glad with her, all ye that love her: rejoice for joy with her, all ye that mourn for her: that ye may suck, and be satisfied with the breasts of her consolations; that ye may milk out, and be delighted with the abundance of her glory. For thus saith the Lord, Behold, I will extend peace to her like a river, and the glory of the Gentiles like a flowing stream: then shall ye suck, ye shall be borne upon her sides, and be dandled upon her knees. As one whom his mother comforteth, so will I comfort you; and ye shall be comforted in Jerusalem.

—Isaiah 66:10–13

At this midpoint in Lent, let us rejoice in our Christian heritage and be thankful for the many blessings in our lives.

READINGS FOR MONDAY

Light snowfall last night reminds me that winter has not yet passed. Perhaps I will spend some time with seed catalogs today and plan our garden.

It is only in that transparency of faith known as humility, in a breath of pure air, that the spirit can live and be discerned.

—*Pierre Talec*

What the spirit brings is very different; love, joy, peace, patience, kindness, goodness, trustfulness, gentleness, and self-control.

—*Galatians 5:22, 23*

Lord, teach us humility so that we may know the fruits of the Spirit.

READINGS FOR TUESDAY

Very cold, windy, and clear. The change in weather is quite a letdown, but hopefully it won't last long. The trees are swaying back and forth in the strong winds that started last night and continue on today.

Faithfulness means continuing quietly with the job we have been given, in the situation where we have been placed; not yielding to the restless desire for change. It means tending the lamp quietly for God without wondering how much longer it has got to go on. Steady unsensational driving, taking good care of the car. A lot of the road to heaven has to be taken at thirty miles per hour. It means keeping everything in your charge in good order for love's sake, rubbing up the silver, polishing the glass even though you know the master will not be looking round the pantry next weekend. If your life is really part of the apparatus of the Spirit, that is the sort of life it must be. You have got to be the sort of cat who can be left alone with the canary: the sort of dog who follows, hungry and thirsty but tail up, to the very end of the day.

—*Evelyn Underhill*

*If we say we have no sin in us,
we are deceiving ourselves
and refusing to admit the truth;
but if we acknowledge our sins,
then God who is faithful and just
will forgive our sins and purify us
from everything that is wrong.*

—1 John 1:8, 9

Lord, help us to see and to admit our sins and shortcomings. Let us grow in faithfulness to you.

READINGS FOR WEDNESDAY

The Bishop was over for the afternoon before a Lenten evensong. I took him across snow-topped muddy fields to see the tree the woodpecker worked over this winter. He commented on the organization of the insects who inhabited the dead tree. We discussed the woodpecker's balance and tenacity in light of this winter's work.

But in this life of companionship with Christ which
we secure by discipline, we find also the surest promise
that we shall discover, each of us, our own
vocation. And here I turn once more to a theme
I have already spoken of; that the duty of any
one of us is—so far as we may—to find out what God
requires of us, and to do it as the work which
God has given us.

—*William Temple*

As the Father has loved me,
So I have loved you.
Remain in my love.
If you keep my commandments
you will remain in my love,

*just as I have kept my Father's commandments
and remain in his love.
I have told you this
so that my own joy may be in you
and your joy be complete.
This is my commandment:
love one another,
as I have loved you.*

—John 15:9–12

Grant us the ability to know our vocation and to live a loving and faithful life, Lord Christ.

READINGS FOR THURSDAY

It's cold and sunny today—a good day for pruning the grapevines. I am reminded that radical pruning can encourage and stimulate new, strong growth.

To live by faith is to pursue quietly and in peace the path on which we are set, in the midst of conflicts and confusions of the creature. In that quiet subordination is fulness of life; not in the passion for self-expression which tries every situation and every relationship and confuses pride with courage and initiative.
—Evelyn Underhill

"Know this too: your kinswoman Elizabeth has, in her old age, herself conceived a son, and she whom people called barren is now in her sixth month, for nothing is impossible to God." "I am the handmaid of the Lord," said Mary, "let what you have said be done to me." And the angel left her.
—Luke 1:36–38

Grant that we may accept our lives as they are in the same gracious way as did Mary, good Lord.

READINGS FOR FRIDAY

Light snow in the morning. Afternoon spent raking the Christmas greens off the flower beds around the house and cutting dead peonies, sweet peas, and other dried flower stalks. An old gardener friend once told me he thought the sweet peas reseeded better if cut in the late winter rather than the fall.

Though we must not look so far off and pry abroad, yet we must be busy near at hand; we must with all arts of the spirit seize upon the present, because it passes from us while we speak, and because in it all our certainty does consist. We must take our waters as out of a torrent and sudden shower, which will quickly cease dropping from above, and quickly cease running in our channels here below; this instant will never return again, and yet it may be this instant will declare or secure the fortune of a whole eternity.

—Jeremy Taylor

To every thing there is a season, and a time to every purpose under the heaven:

a time to be born, and a time to die; a time to plant, and a time to pluck up that which is planted;

> a time to kill, and a time to heal; a time to break down, and a time to build up;
> a time to weep, and a time to laugh; a time to mourn, and a time to dance;
> a time to cast away stones, and a time to gather stones together; a time to embrace, and a time to refrain from embracing;
> a time to get, and a time to lose; a time to keep, and a time to cast away;
> a time to rend, and a time to sew; a time to keep silence, and a time to speak;
> a time to love, and a time to hate; a time of war, and a time of peace.
>
> —Ecclesiastes 3:1–8

Grant us the grace, dear Lord, to understand the times in our lives and to live as if each moment mattered.

READINGS FOR SATURDAY

The sun is warmer—a welcome sight today. Our ancient kitty ventured out for a bit today and seemed to enjoy just "being" in a warm sunny spot.

And remember each day that He who gives you the
morning does not promise you the evening,
and when He gives you the evening there is no
promise to you of the morning. And therefore
spend every moment of the hour according
to the good pleasure of God, and as if no other
time would be given to you; and the more so that for
every moment you must render
the most exact account.
—Dom Lorenzo Scupoli

Teach me to do thy will; for thou art my God: thy Spirit is good; lead me into the land of uprightness.
—*Psalm 143:10*

Help me to remain faithful to your will, your way for me, which is different from that way of my neighbor, dear Lord.

A TIME OF THANKFULNESS
The Fifth Week of Lent

THANKFULNESS

How can we, who live in a time of such advanced technology—where so much can be accomplished so easily by simply pushing a button—learn to be "thankful in little things"? And learning this, how can we remember it? As we observe Lent by prayer, fasting, and almsgiving, reading the Scriptures daily can help us learn to be thankful.

The greatest gift any one of us has is the limitless love our Lord has for us. His Son, Jesus, came to live among us: to show us how to live; to assume the sins of us all; then to die for us so that we might have life eternal. Could there be a greater gift?

Realizing this, what can you do, what can I do to show how thankful we are for our Lord's gift to us? Lent is a good time to meditate on this and to try to make a difference somewhere.

As we have therefore opportunity, let us do good unto all men, especially unto them who are of the household of faith.
—Galatians 6:10

NOW LET US ALL WITH ONE ACCORD

*Now let us all with one accord,
in company with ages past,
keep vigil with our heavenly Lord
in his temptation and his fast.*

*The covenant, so long revealed
to those of faith in former time,
Christ by his own example sealed,
the Lord of love, in love sublime.*

*Your love, O Lord, our sinful race
has not returned, but falsified;
author of mercy, turn your face
and grant repentance for our pride.*

*Remember, Lord, though frail we be,
in your own image were we made;
help us, lest in anxiety,
we cause your Name to be betrayed.*

*Therefore, we pray you, Lord, forgive;
so when our wanderings here shall cease,
we may with you forever live,
in love and unity and peace.*

—Saint Gregory the Great
ca. 540–604

READING FOR SUNDAY

*O give thanks unto the Lord, for he is good:
for his mercy endureth for ever.
Let the redeemed of the Lord say so, whom he hath
redeemed from the hand of the enemy;
and gathered them out of the lands, from the east,
and from the west, from the north, and
from the south.*

*They wandered in the wilderness in a solitary way;
they found no city to dwell in.
Hungry and thirsty, their soul fainted in them.
Then they cried unto the Lord in their trouble, and
he delivered them out of their distresses.
And he led them forth by the right way, that they
might go to a city of habitation.
Oh that men would praise the Lord for his goodness,
and for his wonderful works to the children of
men!
For he satisfieth the longing soul, and filleth
the hungry soul with goodness.*

—Psalm 107:1–9

*Thank you, Lord, for the many blessings that I count.
Let me remember them in times of trouble.*

READINGS FOR MONDAY

Warm and cloudy; rain, maybe snow, is forecast. The last two warmer and sunny days have been wonderful. It makes such a difference just not being cold all the time.

Let us remind ourselves again of God's great promise, that He will treat us as we treat our neighbor. So let us live as we treat our neighbors. So let us be tolerant, considerate, charitable, tender, and sympathetic to our neighbor, and God, faithful to His promise, will do the same for you.
—Jean-Pierre de Caussade

I give you a new commandment:
love one another;
just as I have loved you,
you also must love one another.
By this love you have for one another,
everyone will know that you are my disciples.
—John 13:34–35

Help me to a live a life filled with love and kindness, Lord Christ.

READINGS FOR TUESDAY

Awoke to the birds' chattering this morning, and it was sunny! It is the light that we first notice about the coming of spring—longer days, warmer sunlight—then the bird sounds, especially in the early morning. Saw a robin for the first time this year. Brave little soul! I shall look for the mate later today.

>Dear children, learn to be thankful
>in little things and then you will be able
>to be thankful in great things.
>—Joseph A. Pelletier

Daniel answered and said,
Blessed be the name of God for ever and ever;
　for wisdom and might are his:
and he changeth the times and the seasons:
　he removeth kings, and setteth up kings:
　he giveth wisdom unto the wise,
　　and knowledge to them that know understanding:
he revealeth the deep and secret things:
　he knoweth what is in the darkness,
　and the light dwelleth with him.

I thank thee, and praise thee,
  O thou God of my fathers,
  who hast given me wisdom and might,
  and hast made known unto me now
  what we desired of thee:
  for thou hast now made known unto us
  the king's matter.

—Daniel 2:20–23

For you and your constant love, we give thanks, dear Lord.

READINGS FOR WEDNESDAY

Gray, after a heavy rain in the night, and cooler. The roads are gutted from the rain, and mud season is here. Time for rubber boots.

Suffering is a great mystery. I don't pretend to be able to explain it, but I always feel sure that to follow the way of beauty is to follow the way of truth.

Life itself is such a problem, but there again it can be, and it has been, lifted to loveliness, and that seems to me to be the reason for it. The process makes a product.

If suffering went out of life, courage, tenderness, pity, faith, patience, and love in its divinity would go out of life too. Terrible as suffering is, none the less it is the condition of some of life's very greatest beauties, even as the wounding of the shell is the condition of the pearl's appearing.

I think all of us have to know suffering as life goes on in every part of us. If there is peace, it is not in a part but in the essential self beneath every part. I wish you could look on your Communion as the bringing of your suffering to the perfect Sufferer. I *think* I can say I have known the experience wherein actual suffering became joy, even the dark suffering of the mind and the soul.

I do not pretend to see light, but I do see gleams, and I know I am right to follow those gleams.

—*Father Andrew*

Thy word is a lamp unto my feet, and a light unto my path.

—Psalm 119:105

Grant that we may hear your Word and follow you, Lord Christ.

READINGS FOR THURSDAY

*In spring the great exchange begins,
the exchange between man and nature.
We take action, we give, and
plants promptly respond.*
— Jean Hersey

To rejoice in the midst of a misfortune or seeming sadness, knowing that this may work for good, and will, if we be not wanting to our souls. This is a direct act of hope, to look through the cloud, and look for a beam of the light from God; and this is called in scripture, "rejoicing in tribulation," when "the God of hope fills us with all joy in believing:" every degree of hope brings a degree of joy.
— Jeremy Taylor

*Anyone who claims to be in the light
but hates his brother
is still in the dark.
But anyone who loves his brother is
  living in the light*

*and need not be afraid of stumbling;
unlike the man who hates his brother
    and is in the darkness,
not knowing where he is going,
because it is too dark to see.*

—*1 John 2:9–11*

Lead us in your path of light, good Lord.

READINGS FOR FRIDAY

The weathered tin buckets and clear plastic tubing for collecting sap are up—a sure sign of spring! Our neighbors collect great quantities of sap and produce grade A syrup from the maple trees in the mountains ringing the edges of the valley. While we have several sugar maples, we can't make time for this age-old spring ritual. We do love to buy our valley's syrup at the market in the village and often give it as presents. Twice I have carried it by hand on an airplane trip from the East Coast to the Midwest.

Life is beautiful and the glory of God is immense!
—Paul Claudel

My children,
our love is not to be just words or mere talk,
but something real and active;
only by this can we be certain
that we are children of the truth
and be able to quiet our conscience in his presence,
whatever accusations it may raise against us,
because God is greater than our conscience and he knows everything.

*My dear people,
if we cannot be condemned by our own conscience,
we need not be afraid in God's presence,
and whatever we ask him,
we shall receive,
because we keep his commandments
and live the kind of life that he wants.
His commandments are these:
that we believe in the name of his Son Jesus Christ
and that we love one another
as he told us to.
Whoever keeps his commandments
lives in God and God lives in him.
We know that he lives in us
by the Spirit that he has given us.*

—1 John 3:18–24

Help us to make our love "real and active" and to work to lessen the needs of all those who suffer, Lord Christ.

READINGS FOR SATURDAY

And suddenly all of the snow is gone, including the sprinkling we received this morning, except for a trace on the north side of the knoll. Walking about the place, I see slivers of green in the fields.

God alone can relieve you of your trials. Await His hour patiently. You have always depended too much on human help. God deprives you of it to force you to depend on Him alone, by abandoning yourself solely to His fatherly care.
—Jean-Pierre de Caussade

When the Lord turned again the captivity of Zion,
  we were like them that dream.
Then was our mouth filled with laughter,
  and our tongue with singing:
  then said they among the heathen,
  The Lord hath done great things for them.
The Lord hath done great things for us;
  whereof we are glad.
Turn again our captivity, O Lord,
  as the streams in the south.

They that sow in tears
　　shall reap in joy.
He that goeth forth and weepeth,
　　bearing precious seed,
　　shall doubtless come again with rejoicing,
　　bringing his sheaves with him.
　　　　　　　　　　　　　—Psalm 126

When the time comes to "sow in tears," let us remember your promise of "reaping in joy," dear Lord.

A TIME FOR CHANGE
PALM SUNDAY AND HOLY WEEK

CHANGE

Lent is a time for change. As we observe Palm Sunday and Holy Week we near the conclusion of our Lenten observance. During this week we recall the institution of the Last Supper and the Crucifixion. In meditating on Jesus' surrender on the cross and his acceptance of God's will for him, let us surrender to the cross in our daily lives and live with acceptance of that of which we formerly would most have wanted to be rid. Surrender and acceptance lead to change—a life filled with new vision, new perspective. These can help us to give up our old ways and to move ahead with hope, knowing that we are not alone. The One who has gone before also goes along with us.

As all of nature is giving signs of new life, so we, too, will give signs of our new life. We can shed the wrappings of darkness and winter and celebrate the lengthening of days. At the end of Holy Week, preparations for the celebration of Easter Day take over the house. There's much to be done to show outwardly that we have put aside the works of darkness and put on the armor of light (Rom. 13:12).

Some of the many ways we can prepare for the celebration of Easter follow: give the house a good spring cleaning; make a special flower arrangement of forsythia, pussy willow, or some other spring-blooming plants; bake Kulich or other Easter cakes; plan an Easter feast to break the Lenten fast with family or friends; and color or decorate eggs. All of these symbolic acts give witness to the new life we are experiencing inwardly.

ALL GLORY, LAUD, AND HONOR

    All glory, laud, and honor
    To thee, Redeemer, King!
    To whom the lips of children
    Made sweet hosannas ring.

Thou art the King of Israel, Thou
    David's royal Son,
Who in the Lord's Name comest,
    The King and Blessed One.
    All glory, laud, and honor
    To thee, Redeemer, King!
    To whom the lips of children
    Made sweet hosannas ring.

The company of angels are praising thee on high;
And mortal men, and all things Created, make reply.
    All glory, laud, and honor
    To thee, Redeemer, King!
    To whom the lips of children
    Made sweet hosannas ring.

The people of the Hebrews with palms before thee went;
Our praise and prayers and anthems before thee we present.
    All glory, laud, and honor
    To thee, Redeemer, King!
    To whom the lips of children
    Made sweet hosannas ring.

To thee, before thy passion, They sang their hymns of praise;
To thee, now high exalted, Our melody we raise.
    All glory, laud, and honor
    To thee Redeemer, King!
    To whom the lips of children
    Made sweet hosannas ring.

Thou didst accept their praises; Accept the prayers we bring,
Who in all good delightest, Thou good and gracious King.
    All glory, laud, and honor
    To thee, Redeemer, King!
    To whom the lips of children
    Made sweet hosannas ring.

                        —Saint Theodulph
                                750–ca. 821
           (Translated by John Mason Neale, 1854)

READING FOR PALM SUNDAY

*His state was divine,
yet he did not cling
to his equality with God
but emptied himself
to assume the condition of a slave,
and became as men are;
and being as all men are,
he was humbler yet,
even to accepting death,
death on a cross.
But God raised him high
and gave him the name
which is above all other names
so that all beings
in the heavens, on earth and in the underworld,
should bend the knee at the name of Jesus
and that every tongue should acclaim
Jesus Christ as Lord,
to the glory of God the Father.*

—Philippians 2:6–11

Grant that at the name of Jesus we may remember his humility and his acceptance of God's will and that in remembering we may be changed.

READINGS FOR MONDAY

Drove across three counties today and passed several hawks cruising the gray, winterlike sky—few raindrops, few snowflakes. There were slivers of shiny, fat, budding pussy willows along the roadside. The willow trees are showing a new, fresh yellow-green.

Only the Lord carried his cross completely alone. Everyone who follows him in carrying his cross does so within the community of saints in heaven.

—Adrienne von Speyr

The Spirit of the Lord God is upon me; because the Lord hath anointed me to preach good tidings unto the meek; he hath sent me to bind up the brokenhearted, to proclaim liberty to the captives, and the opening of the prison to them that are bound; to proclaim the acceptable year of the Lord, and the day of vengeance of our God; to comfort all that mourn. . . .

—Isaiah 61:1–2

As we pick up our crosses and carry them, let us never lose sight of the One who went before us.

READINGS FOR TUESDAY

Sunny but coolish. More rain expected tonight. Ahead, another day of raking and cleaning up the debris of winter. The garlic, planted last October, is showing green.

What about the dreadful moment when a great test of courage, great suffering, a great bereavement faced us and we knew we were for it and found the agony was more than we could face? The revelation that someone we trusted could not be trusted any more, that someone loved profit better than they loved us? How do we feel when we have to suffer for someone else's wrongdoing? How do we bear mockery and contempt, especially if it is directed at our religious life or at the unfortunate discrepancy between our religious life and our character? What about the sting, the lash, of humiliation or disappointment, the unfortunate events that stripped us of the seamless drapery of self-respect and convention and left us naked to the world; the wounds given by those we loved best; the loneliness inseparable from some phase of the spiritual life. All this happens over and over again. Can we weave it all into the sacrifice of love?

Here again Christ does not go outside our ordinary condition. He hallows real life. Can we hallow it? Can we bear to let the light of the window fall on our little fears, humiliations and pains and endure the chemical rays which can transform them into part of His sacrifice? Can we weave all that into the sacrifice of love, and what are we going to do with it if we can't? Our world is chaos without the Cross; for we

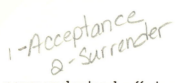

never understand suffering until we have embraced it, turned it into sacrifice and given ourselves in it to God.

—*Evelyn Underhill*

Fear thou not; for I am with thee: be not dismayed; for I am thy God: I will strengthen thee; yea, I will help thee; yea, I will uphold thee with the right hand of my righteousness.

—*Isaiah 41:10*

Strengthen me for the tasks ahead, Lord Christ.

READINGS FOR WEDNESDAY

Walked out South Street to hear the peepers, and heard just one peeper, sounding over and over again under stars shining with the crystal ice of spring. What courage it must take, when nobody else has waked up yet!
—Viola White

In the shadow of your mercy
we shelter, O Mother of God.
Do not ignore our supplications
in our temptation,
but deliver us from danger,
o pure one, blessed one.
—Byzantine divine office, third century

One of the elders then spoke, and asked me, "Do you know who these people are, dressed in white robes, and where they have come from?" I answered him, "You can tell me, my lord." Then he said, "These are the people who have been through the great persecution, and because they have washed their robes white again in the blood of the Lamb, they now stand in front of God's throne and

serve him day and night in his sanctuary; and the One who sits on the throne will spread his tent over them. They will never hunger or thirst again; neither the sun nor scorching wind will ever plague them, because the Lamb who is at the throne will be their shepherd and will lead them to springs of living water; and God will wipe away all tears from their eyes."

—Revelations 7:13–17

Strengthen our faith and trust in you, Lord Christ.

MAUNDY THURSDAY

On the Thursday preceding Easter, we celebrate our Lord's Last Supper. Jesus and the twelve apostles were gathered together to celebrate the Passover. Because Jesus washed the feet of his disciples before the meal, it has long been the custom to observe foot-washing, known as *Pedilavium*, during which twelve people come forward to have their feet washed by the celebrant on this day. The name Maundy Thursday comes from the Latin *mandatum novum* (new commandment), which is pronounced at the beginning of the ceremony (see John 13:34 or the reading for Monday on p. 74).

This night commemorates the betrayal of Jesus and his institution of the Holy Eucharist.

When the hour came he took his place at table, and the apostles with him. And he said to them, "I have longed to eat this passover with you before I suffer; because, I tell you, I shall not eat it again until it is fulfilled in the kingdom of God."

Then, taking a cup, he gave thanks and said, "Take this and share it among you, because from now on, I tell you, I shall not drink wine until the kingdom of God comes."

Then he took some bread and when he had given thanks, broke it and gave it to them, saying, "This is my body which will be given for you; do this as a memorial of me." He did the same with the cup after supper, and said, "This cup is the new covenant in my blood which will be poured out for you."

—Luke 22:14–22

We celebrate the Holy Eucharist regularly today as a reenactment of that Last Supper.

On Maundy Thursday, either purple (violet) or white vestments are worn. Immediately following the service, the consecrated bread—to be used for Good Friday's Mass of the Presanctified—is taken to the altar of repose or to the tabernacle where a vigil is kept. Afterwards, the altar is stripped, and holy water containers emptied in preparation for Good Friday. Other liturgical acts of the day include blessing of the holy oils and the reconciliation of penitents.

Other names for Maundy Thursday include Sheer Thursday (perhaps from *skere* or *sheer*, meaning "clean, free from guilt," in reference to the absolution received or to the washing of altars on that day) and Green Thursday (from the Latin *dies viridium*, "green day," the German name for this day). This name may come from the distribution of green branches to those who confessed on Ash Wednesday, as a token that their penance was complete.

TENEBRAE

Tenebrae, meaning "darkness," is a service of mattins and lauds provided for the last three days of Holy Week. Fifteen candles provide the only light in the church. They are extinguished, one after each reading of a psalm during the service, until the church is in darkness.

READINGS FOR MAUNDY THURSDAY

Surprise snowfall in the night! There is green grass peeping through the lawn cover. I picked a dozen or so daffodils after breakfast. Their cups were snow-filled. The birds are quieter than usual: all of nature is a bit surprised, myself included.

Wash me, therefore, O my Jesus, from all the filth of my sins, cleanse me from every defilement, whether of body or of soul so that, being made clean from head to foot, I may be found meet to have part with you, in that everlasting joy, which you have promised to all your loved ones, who in times of temptation have held fast to you.

Give me also, I pray you, an understanding heart, that I may be able fully to comprehend that most sweet discourse, which you spoke at the Supper: for its words are indeed words breathing most fervent love, the sweetest comfort, and the most exalted wisdom. So write your new commandment upon the tables of my heart, that my soul may be on fire with the twofold love which it enjoins: strengthen me in every trouble that may come upon me, and in place of this world's joys, fill me with the most sweet comfort of your Holy Spirit.

—Thomas à Kempis

A dispute arose also between them about which should be reckoned the greatest, but he said to them, "Among pagans it is the kings who lord it over them, and those who have authority over them are given the title Benefactor. This must not happen with you. No; the greatest among you must behave as if he were the youngest, the leader as if he were the one who serves. For who is the greater: the one at table or the one who serves? The one at table, surely? Yet here am I among you as one who serves!"

—Luke 22:24–27

Let us remember, Lord Christ, you are One who serves. May we as followers of you also serve.

GOOD FRIDAY

Good Friday, the day of Christ's crucifixion, is the most solemn day in the church year. A day of fast, abstinence, and penance, its liturgical color, formerly black, is now red. This day and Holy Saturday are the only days of the year when no celebration of the eucharist takes place. In places where Holy Communion is to be administered, the presanctified elements from Maundy Thursday are used. Many churches have three-hour services from noon to 3:00 P.M., the hours that Christ died on the cross.

There is a tradition, dating back several centuries in England, of people eating hot cross buns for breakfast on this day.

READINGS FOR GOOD FRIDAY

ALONE THOU GOEST FORTH, O LORD

Alone thou goest forth, O Lord,
  In sacrifice to die;
Is this thy sorrow naught to us
  Who pass unheeding by?

Our sins, not thine, thou bearest, Lord,
  Make us thy sorrow feel,
Till through our pity and our shame
  Love answers love's appeal.

This is earth's darkest hour, but thou
  Dost light and life restore;
Then let all praise be given thee
  Who livest evermore.

Give us compassion for thee, Lord,
  That, as we share this hour,
Thy cross may bring us to thy joy
  And resurrection power. Amen.

—Peter Abelard, 1079–1142

Grant that I may now make a fresh start, c
follow you, not with the infirmity of purpos
who are neither hot nor cold, but with ren
fervor of heart; keeping my eyes steadily fixed upon
you, the Cross-bearer, and not letting them stray
hither and thither like those who are inconstant in
their ways. Be my guide along the narrow road, and
my companion as I follow it: be at hand to help me
when things are going well with me, to comfort me
when they are going wrong, to sustain me in all the
trials which I may have to undergo for the sake of
your holy name.

—*Thomas à Kempis*

In all our experiences we are being taken apart by our Lord to learn about Him. If we do it in union with Him, pain is transfigured to Sacrifice, work to service. Jesus first prayed to know His Father's will, then made His choice, the Cross. In doing His Father's will Love transfigures Him.

—*Father Andrew*

> Pray for God's will for me

He is despised and rejected of men; a man of sorrows, and acquainted with grief: and we hid as it

were our faces from him; he was despised, and we esteemed him not.

Surely he hath borne our griefs, and carried our sorrows: yet we did esteem him stricken, smitten of God, and afflicted. But he was wounded for our transgressions, he was bruised for our iniquities: the chastisement of our peace was upon him; and with his stripes we are healed. All we like sheep have gone astray; we have turned every one to his own way; and the Lord hath laid on him the iniquity of us all.

—Isaiah 53:3–6

Grant that by your suffering and sacrifice we may be healed, Lord Christ.

STATIONS OF THE CROSS

The stations of the cross, also known as "the way of the cross," is a service based on fourteen artistic images—pictures, carvings, ceramic pieces—depicting incidents in the last journey of Jesus from Pilate's house to the entombment. Designed for devotional purposes, they are often hung in churches and used especially in Lent. The devotion is thought to have come from pilgrims visiting Jerusalem and following the traditional route from Pilate's house to Calvary. The stations commemorate the following events:

1. Jesus is condemned to death.

2. Jesus takes up his cross.

3. Jesus falls the first time.

4. Jesus meets his mother.

5. The cross is laid on Simon of Cyrene.

6. A woman, Veronica, wipes the face of Jesus.

7. Jesus falls a second time.

8. Jesus meets the women of Jerusalem.

9. Jesus falls a third time.

10. Jesus is stripped of his garments.

11. Jesus is nailed to the cross.

12. Jesus dies on the cross.

13. The body of Jesus is taken down from the cross.

14. Jesus is laid in the tomb.

HOLY SATURDAY

Also known as Easter Even, this day commemorates the descent of Jesus into Hades. "I praise and honour you, O most gracious Jesus, for mercifully visiting in Limbo the saints of the old dispensation, and for releasing all the faithful souls which were resting in Abraham's bosom," in the words of Thomas à Kempis.

READINGS FOR HOLY SATURDAY

The spring peepers have started their nocturnal chorus. Crocuses and daffodils are blooming, and buds are on the tulips. All of nature sings alleluia.

They indeed had for a long time anxiously looked for your descent into Hades, and with eyes full of tears were lovingly exclaiming, as we do now in this days' processional: "Thou art come, O loved One, whom we have long waited for in our darkness; thou art this night come to bring forth from the prison house those who were bound."

—Thomas à Kempis

In thee, O Lord, do I put my trust; let me never be ashamed: deliver me in thy righteousness. Bow down thine ear to me; deliver me speedily: be thou my strong rock, for a house of defense to save me.

For thou art my rock, and my fortress; therefore for thy name's sake lead me, and guide me.

*Pull me out of the net that they have laid privily for me: for thou art my strength.
Into thine hand I commit my spirit: thou hast redeemed me, O Lord God of truth.*

—Psalm 31:1–5

Lead me through the darkness to the light of your Truth, Lord Christ.

PASCHAL VIGIL SERVICE

The paschal vigil service, the principal celebration of Easter, is observed between sunset on Holy Saturday and sunrise on Easter morning. The service normally is composed of four parts: the service of light, the service of lessons, baptism or the renewal of baptismal vows, and the Holy Eucharist.

In the darkness of the church, the new fire is kindled; from this fire the paschal candle is lighted with the celebrant's saying, "The Light of Christ." The service of lessons includes nine readings from the Psalms and Old Testament. Renewal of baptismal vows and baptism (if any) follows. The service concludes with the celebration of the Easter eucharist.

EASTER IS HERE

CELEBRATE

Let us celebrate in every way we can this glorious day of our Lord's resurrection. But behind our outward trappings, festive though they may be, may our hearts be changed and ready for new life in the knowledge of his conquering death.

Signs of new life abound as we see and hear the awakening of the earth, and of life, from the mantle of winter. Children anxious to celebrate this day will be hunting colored eggs and merry-making. We, too, in the knowledge of our Lord's redemptive love for us, will hasten our step as we move to our churches to sing the familiar hymns and observe this great Christian festival, our Lord's triumph over the pains of death and the grave, the return of Light in our lives.

HAIL THEE, FESTIVAL DAY!

Hail thee, festival day!
Blest day that art hallowed for ever;
Day whereon Christ arose,
breaking the kingdom of death.

Lo, the fair beauty of earth,
from the death of the winter arising!
Ev'ry good gift of the year
now with its Master returns:

Hail thee, festival day!
Blest day that art hallowed for ever;
Day whereon Christ arose,
breaking the kingdom of death.

He who was nailed to the cross
is Lord and the ruler of all men;
All things created on earth
sing to the glory of God:

(Chorus)

Daily the loveliness grows,
adorned with the glory of blossom;
Heaven her gates unbars,
flinging her increase of light:

(Chorus)

Rise from the grave now, O Lord,
who art author of life and creation.
Treading the pathway of death,
life thou bestowest on man:

(Chorus)

God the All-Father, the Lord,
who rulest the earth and the heavens,
Guard us from harm without,
cleanse us from evil within:

(Chorus)

Jesus the health of the world,
enlighten our minds, thou Redeemer,
Son of the Father supreme,
only begotten of God:

(Chorus)

Spirit of life and of power,
now flow in us, fount of our being,
Light that dost lighten all,
life that in all dost abide:

(Chorus)

Praise to the Giver of good!
Thou love who art author of concord,
Pour out thy balm on our souls,
order our ways in thy peace:

Hail thee, festival day!
blest day that art hallowed for ever;
Day whereon Christ arose,
breaking the kingdom of death.

—Venantius Honorius Fortunatus, 530–609

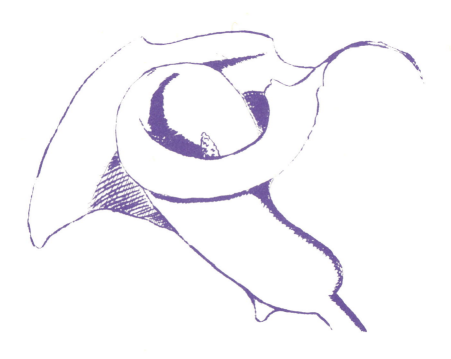

EASTER

Easter, the feast of the resurrection of Christ, is the greatest and oldest feast of the Christian year. A movable feast with a different date each year, Easter falls on the first Sunday after the first full moon of the spring equinox. The limits of the paschal moon are 21 March and 25 April.

Christ is risen; he is risen indeed! The *Alleluia* is restored to the service; liturgical vestments are white. All the Christian world focuses on the return to life and hope of the Risen One.

Probably, the early celebrations of Easter developed from the Jewish Passover rite. According to Bede, Easter is related to the Anglo-Saxon spring goddess Eostre. As with the celebration of Christmas, that of Easter has origins in ancient times.

Today we always think of brightly colored eggs, baskets delivered by an Easter bunny, and lilies at Easter. Long before the time of Christ, eggs were symbols of life and rebirth. It is said that ancient Greeks, Romans, Persians, and Chinese exchanged eggs as gifts at spring festivals. The Eastern Christian church has a great tradition of decorating eggs. Some churches in the West have a blessing of the eggs on Easter day. Coloring Easter eggs is a tradition in many households today.

The tradition of Easter baskets in this country is said to have come from German settlers in the early eighteenth century who told their children that rabbits brought colored eggs. The children then made grass nests, which were later replaced by baskets.

Easter lilies, plants originating in the Far East, began to be cultivated here during World War II when supplies from Japan were cut off. Their lovely fragrance fills many churches and homes throughout Eastertide. After enjoying a lily in the house or church, try planting the bulbs when the foliage has died back. Surprisingly enough, even in our cold northern climes, the lilies, when properly insulated by snow, will bloom for many seasons—but much later than Easter day.

Sunrise services on Easter day are a tradition in the United States and in some parts of Europe. I recall my mother's telling of her childhood in Winston-Salem, North Carolina. Thousands followed a procession through the town to attend the Moravian sunrise service in Old Salem. It must have been a moving experience as the people processed through the town accompanied by the Moravian band of wind instruments divided into groups playing antiphonally. The service was held in the graveyard amidst the flat tombstones at daybreak.

Special foods are related to Easter as Christians break the Lent-long fast. Roasted spring lamb, breads and cakes of many types and shapes are part of the feast that is celebrated at home on this holy day. In the South, one often sees cake baked in the shape of a lamb frosted with a fresh coconut icing. A Finnish Easter bread celebrating both Easter and the arrival of spring is traditionally baked in milking pails to celebrate the arrival of new calves. The recipe for Kulich, a Russian Easter bread, can be found on page 120.

READINGS FOR EASTER DAY

As we walked into the damp coolness of St. Timothy's church early this morning, the fragrance of blooming lilies permeated every part of our senses. The weeks of preparation and waiting were over. Easter, at last!

The stone which the builders refused is
   become the head stone of the corner.
This is the Lord's doing; it is
   marvelous in our eyes.
This is the day which the Lord hath made;
   we will rejoice and be glad in it.
—Psalm 118:22–24

On the first day of the week, at the first sign of dawn, they went to the tomb with the spices they had prepared. They found that the stone had been rolled away from the tomb, but on entering discovered that the body of the Lord Jesus was not there. As they stood there not knowing what to think, two men in brilliant clothes suddenly appeared at their side. Terrified, the women lowered their eyes. But the two men said to them, "Why look among the

dead for someone who is alive? He is not here; he has risen. Remember what he told you when he was still in Galilee: that the Son of Man had to be handed over into the power of sinful men and be crucified, and rise again on the third day." And they remembered his words.

When the women returned from the tomb, they told all this to the Eleven and to all the others. The women were Mary of Magdala, Joanna, and Mary the mother of James.

—Luke 24:1–10

Alleluia. Christ is risen. The Lord is risen indeed. Alleluia.

Seasonal Recipes

SIMNEL CAKE

Simnel cake (from the old French *simenel*, from the Latin *simila*) gets its name from the word meaning the finest wheat flour. Some describe it as a rich plum cake enclosed in a hard dough crust, some say it is a currant cake, and some insist it has a marzipan frosting. There are probably as many variations of simnel cake as there are imaginative cooks who add a special "something" from their cupboard. The following recipe is delicious and very easy to make. Try making it to enjoy with your family and friends or to take to church and share at coffee hour.

Simnel Cake

1½	cups flour	½	cup currants
½	tsp. baking powder	1	cup chopped candied fruits such as cherries and pineapple slices
¼	tsp. allspice		
¼	tsp. cinnamon		
¼	tsp. nutmeg	2	tbls. mixed candied fruit peel
¼	tsp. ground cloves	3	eggs beaten lightly
¼	cup softened butter	½	tsp. vanilla
¾	cup sugar	2	tbls. brandy
¾	cup golden raisins		OVEN: 300°

1. Mix raisins, currants, candied fruits, and candied peel with 1 tablespoon flour and set aside.

2. Sift remaining flour, baking powder, allspice, cinnamon, nutmeg, and cloves and set aside.

3. In a large bowl, cream butter and sugar together until light. Beat in eggs, brandy, and vanilla. A food processor or electric mixer may be used.

4. Beat in flour mix gradually until just combined.

5. Add the fruit and peel mix to the batter and combine well.

119

6. Turn the batter into a greased layer-cake pan and press down the surface with the back of a spoon to smooth.

7. Bake 1¼ to 1½ hours or until a cake tester inserted in the center comes out clean.

8. Let cool before removing from pan and cool completely before frosting.

Frosting: Beat ⅓ cup softened butter until light. Gradually beat in 3½ cups confectioners' sugar until fluffy. Beat in 2 teaspoons vanilla and about 3 tablespoons milk until smooth. If it seems too thick, add a little more milk.

KULICH

On top of this tall, cylindrical Easter bread, Russian Orthodox housewives put the initials XB (resembling the Cyrillic letters XR), which stand for the words *Christ is risen.* The initials are made of colored icing, candied fruit, or raisins. Traditionally, you should slice this bread horizontally. First, cut off the top. Remove the slices to be served. Then put the top piece back on the loaf, like a hat. Eat the top with the last slice.

Kulich

1	package dry yeast	1	egg
¼	cup warm water (105°–115°)	½	cup raisins
		½	cup citron or candied fruit
½	cup lukewarm milk (scalded then cooled)	2	tbls. chopped almonds
		½	tsp. grated lemon peel
¼	cup butter, melted		about 3 cups flour
½	tsp. salt (can omit)		
¼	cup sugar OVEN: 375°	2	1 lb. coffee cans or 1 46-oz. juice can

1. In a large bowl, dissolve yeast in warm water.

2. Scald milk. Add butter to it to melt. Cool mixture to lukewarm. Add to yeast mixture.

3. Stir in sugar, salt, egg, raisins, citron, almonds, and lemon peel.

4. Add 2 cups flour. Stir until smooth. Gradually stir in enough remaining flour to make dough manageable.

5. Turn dough onto lightly floured surface and knead for about 5 minutes or until smooth.

6. Place in large greased bowl. Turn the dough over so that it is greased on both sides. Cover bowl with plastic wrap and let rise in warm place until double, 1 to 1½ hours.

7. Punch down dough and divide into halves. Place in two well-greased 1-pound coffee cans—or large juice can, which I prefer—and let rise until double, 40–50 minutes.

8. Place baking sheet on a low rack and heat oven to 375°. Place can or cans on baking sheet and bake for 40 minutes. Cool for 10 minutes before removing bread from can. (Opening other end of can makes removing bread easier!) Spoon on icing and add XB.

Icing. Mix ½ cup powdered sugar, 1 teaspoon warm water, and 1 teaspoon lemon juice until smooth. Spoon over warm kulich. Allow some to drizzle down sides.

Saints' Days
During Lent

6 FEBRUARY
The Martyrs of Japan
1597

St. Francis Xavier established a Christian mission in Japan in 1549; the Jesuits were soon followed by the Franciscans. During this time many Japanese were converted to Christianity. The authorities, fearing the missions were preparatory to Western conquest, attempted to suppress them and began to persecute the Christians. The twenty-six people martyred on a hill near Nagasaki—six Franciscan friars, three Jesuits, and their converts who refused to recant—suffered crucifixion for their faith in 1597. Quite remarkably, many years later, a Christian faith, descended from these early missions, was discovered. In the Anglican Church, the day commemorating their martyrdom is observed on 5 February.

10 FEBRUARY
Saint Scholastica
ca. 480–ca. 543

What we know of St. Scholastica of Nursia comes from St. Gregory's Dialogues. Tradition says that St. Scholastica established a convent near Monte Cassino, where her twin brother, St. Benedict, lived with a small band of monks. Nearby, sister and brother would meet once a year for prayer and talk. The legend of St. Scholastica says that toward the end of her life, after a day of talking about the spiritual life and praying with St. Benedict, Scholastica, seeing that it was time for him to leave, asked her brother to stay the night and continue talking. St. Benedict, mindful of the order's rule that he not pass a night away from his monastery, said he could not. She turned to God in prayer and suddenly a lightning storm arose. He then had no choice but to stay. St. Scholastica is said to have died three days later. Her name is invoked against storms.

11 FEBRUARY
Our Lady of Lourdes
1858

On 11 February 1858, a vision of the Blessed Virgin Mary appeared to a fourteen-year-old French peasant girl, Bernadette Soubirous (later St. Bernadette Soubirous, 1844–1879), in the grotto of a rock at Lourdes in the Hautés Pyrénées of France. This site, where a spring appeared, has become a place of pilgrimage associated with many miraculous healings.

24 FEBRUARY
Saint Matthias, the Apostle
First Century

As told in Acts 1:15–26, Matthias, who had been with the followers of Jesus throughout his ministry, was chosen by lot to become one of the Twelve to fill the vacancy left by the traitor, Judas Iscariot. Some say he started his ministry in Judea but later went to other lands. The Greeks say he planted the faith in Cappadocia (eastern Turkey) and on the Caspian coast. Legendary sources say he was martyred. A lost apocryphal Gospel is called the Gospel of St. Matthias. The feast day for St. Matthias in the Anglican Church is 24 February. Elsewhere in the Western world it is 14 May; in the Greek church, 9 August.

7 MARCH
Saint Perpetua and Her Companions
203

Vibia Perpetua (a young, well-born, married mother of an infant) and her companions (among whom was the slave Felicitas) were slain in the amphitheater at

Carthage in Africa in A.D. 203 for confessing the name of Christ. After being attacked by a savage cow, she was killed by the sword of a gladiator on the nones of March, nonis Martii.

St. Perpetua rejected the pleas of her elderly father to save herself on behalf of him and her infant child. Instead she chose to follow her Lord in his Passion and death, witnessing to the Way, the Truth, the Life. Renouncing the name Christian and making sacrifices to the Roman gods for the prosperity of the emperor were sufficient proof that one was not an enemy of the state. But Saints Perpetua and Felicity and their companions rejected idolatry: they chose martyrdom instead.

During her confinement in prison, Perpetua kept a diary, which is one of the earliest documents of the Church. Firsthand impressions of arrest and imprisonment are written in her own hand.

9 MARCH
Saint Gregory, Bishop of Nyssa
ca. 334–ca.395

Born in Caesarea, Cappadocia, in a family of ten, Gregory was ordained bishop by his brother Basil the Great, bishop of Caesarea. Philosopher and theologian, a scholar by nature, he is highly esteemed for his writings, most of which survive today. His writing on the Trinity was important in developing the doctrine of the Trinity. The following is from a homily of St. Gregory's on the Annunciation:

Hail, O full of grace . . . I weep no more, I grieve no more, nor do I speak: In my palm, I do not twist in piercing thorns, for the Lord has taken the thorns from our sins crowning his own head; my sin has vanished, my old calamity dissolved, the tree of life and grace flourishes through the Holy Virgin. . . .

St. Gregory attended the Council of Constantinople in 381, the second ecumenical council.

12 March
Saint Gregory the Great
540–604

St. Gregory the Great, considered the father of the medieval papacy, served during a time of plague, famine, and barbaric invasion. He was not only an able administrator who managed to spend vast sums of money on charity but also a prolific author. A hymn of his, "Kind Maker of the World, O Hear," is included on p. 44 of this book. The Dialogues was one of the most popular books of the Middle Ages. His Regula Pastoralis, a book on the office of bishop, was translated into English during the reign of King Alfred the Great, who gave a copy to each of his bishops. Even today with its insistance on the bishop as, most of all, a physician of souls whose chief duties are preaching and the enforcement of discipline, the book is considered important.

The ordering of church liturgy and development of liturgical music (plainsong/Gregorian chant) of his time imprints the Western church still.

A noted preacher in the churches of Rome, St. Gregory liked to preach basing his homilies on the Gospel of the day. Many of these remain. From his own monastery of St. Andrew, which he had founded early in his career at his family home, he chose Augustine and forty missionaries and sent them to Britain to evangelize and convert the Anglo-Saxon world.

The title he assumed for his pontificate, Servus servorum Dei (Servant of the servants of God) exemplifies both his great humility and his many accomplishments as Pope Gregory I.

17 March
Saint Patrick, Archbishop of Armagh
ca. 389–ca. 461

Born of Christian parents of Romano-British origin, Patrick's life became the source of many legends. At around sixteen, he was captured by Irish pirates and taken to Ireland, where he was held in slavery for six years. Attributing his escape and return to Britain to miraculous powers, Patrick returned much changed. It is thought that he received training for the ministry in France and returned to Ireland as bishop to evangelize. He spent the remainder of his life there. In less than thirty years, Patrick converted Ireland as a whole to Christianity.

St. Patrick wrote a moving account of his spiritual pilgrimage, which is called Confession. The Lorica, or Deer's Cry or St. Patrick's Breastplate, is also attributed to him. While it may or may not have been written by him, it does, nevertheless, characterize the period in which he lived.

I bind unto myself today
The strong Name of the Trinity,
By invocation of the same,
The Three in One, and One in Three. . . .

Christ be with me, Christ within me,
Christ behind me, Christ before me,
Christ beside me, Christ to win me,
Christ to comfort and restore me,
Christ beneath me, Christ above me,
Christ in quiet, Christ in danger,
Christ in hearts of all that love me,
Christ in mouth of friend and stranger.

The legend of the shamrock and St. Patrick's use of its tripartite shape to explain the Trinity to the two daughters of the pagan King Laoghaire has long been associated with this saint.

18 MARCH
Saint Cyril, Archbishop of Jerusalem
ca. 315–386

Cyril grew up in Jerusalem in a family that was most likely Christian. He received an excellent education.

The Catecheses, which were delivered as instruction for baptismal candidates in Lent for baptism on Holy Saturday, are his chief surviving work. They give a good picture of fourth-century liturgical practices.

During this time of bitter religious controversy, St. Cyril spent sixteen of the thirty-five years of his episcopate in exile. In 381, he attended the Council of Constantinople, at which the amended form of the Nicene Creed was promulgated.

19 MARCH
Saint Joseph
First Century

Fragments of St. Joseph's story are told in the infancy narratives of Matthew and Luke. He is present at our Lord's presentation in the Temple, at his placement in the arms of Simeon, and when our Lord, at twelve, was found talking with the doctors in the Temple (see Luke 2).

A pious Jew, descended from David, he was from Bethlehem. A carpenter by trade, Joseph is best known as spouse of the Blessed Virgin Mary. We assume that Jesus spent his formative early years in his household, but at the marriage at Cana (John 2) when "the mother of Jesus was there," there is no mention of Joseph.

St. Joseph is invoked as the patron of a happy death.

25 MARCH
The Annunciation of Our Lord Jesus Christ
to the Blessed Virgin Mary

"Lady Day" commemorates the announcement by the angel Gabriel to the Virgin: "Mary, do not be afraid; you have won God's favor. Listen! You are to conceive and bear a son, and you must name him Jesus. He will be great and will be called Son of the Most High. The Lord God will give him the throne of his ancestor David; he will rule over the House of Jacob for ever and his reign will have no end" (Luke 1:31–35).

19 APRIL
Saint Alphege, Archbishop of Canterbury
1012

Alphege entered the monastic life as a young man and for a short time lived as a solitary near Bath, in Britain. At thirty he became bishop of Winchester. It was said that he gave so liberally to the poor that there were no beggars in the diocese of Winchester during his twenty-two-year episcopate.

St. Alphege succeeded Archbishop Aelfric as archbishop of Canterbury. During this time, invading Danes laid seige to Canterbury. St. Alphege hastened to the center of the struggle and was captured. Saying the country was too poor to pay a high ransom for him, St. Alphege accepted death by the Danes. His death, for the sake of justice, has always been regarded as martyrdom by the English.

Notes

Introduction

Shrove Tuesday

. . . demonic power. Joseph Cardinal Ratzinger, *Seek That Which Is Above* (San Francisco: Ignatius Press, 1986), 31.

Ash Wednesday

. . . shall return. *The Book of Common Prayer* of the Protestant Episcopal Church (New York: Seabury Press, 1979), 265.

A Time of Acceptance

Monday

. . . are frosted . . . Viola White, *Vermont Diary* (Boston: Charles T. Branford Company, 1956), 1.

. . . to light." Pierre Talec, *Jesus and the Hunger for Things Unknown* (New York: Seabury Press, 1982), 22.

Tuesday

. . . once more. White, *Vermont Dairy*, 6–7.

. . . of Love. Father Andrew, *The Life and Letters of Father Andrew, S.D.C.*, Treasures from the Spiritual Classics (Wilton, CT: Morohouse Publishing, 1982), 60.

Wednesday

. . . with Him. Andrew, *Life and Letters*, 36.

Thursday

. . . free path! Evelyn Underhill, *Light of Christ*, Treasures from the Spiritual Classics (Wilton, CT: Morehouse Publishing, 1982), 43–44.

131

Friday

. . . of life. Joseph the Studite, in Berselli and Gharib, *Sing the Joys of Mary*, 113, hymn 86.

Saturday

. . . new life. Talec, *Jesus*, 37–38.

A Time of Repentance

Monday

. . . to him. Joseph A. Pelletier, *The Queen of Peace Visits Medugorje* (Worcester, MA: Assumption Press, 1985), 210.

Tuesday

. . . enrich us. Jean-Pierre de Caussade, *Spiritual Letters*, trans. Kitty Muggeridge (Wilton, CT: Morehouse Publishing, 1986), 87.

Wednesday

. . . to pray. Pelletier, *Queen of Peace*, 182.

Thursday

. . . and fast. Saint Anselm, *The Prayers and Meditations of Saint Anselm with the Proslogio*, trans. Sister Benedicta Ward, S.L.G. (New York: Viking Penguin, 1973), 11.89–99, 242.

Friday

. . . right place. William Temple, *Christian Faith and Life*, Treasures from the Spiritual Classics (Wilton, CT: Morehouse Publishing, 1982), 30.

Saturday

. . . and me. James Russell Lowell, "The Vision of Sir Launfal," part 2. st. 8 (1848).

A Time of Obedience

Monday

. . . of God. de Caussade, *Spiritual Letters*, 33.

Tuesday

. . . of fruitfulness. Adrienne von Speyr, *Handmaid of the Lord*, trans. E.A. Nelson (San Francisco: Ignatius Press, 1985), 7.

Wednesday

. . . to give. Talec, *Jesus*, 72.

Thursday

. . . the heart. Underhill, *Light of Christ*, 37.

Friday

. . . the Mother. von Speyr, *Handmaid of the Lord*, 27.

Saturday

. . . to it. de Caussade, *Spiritual Letters*, 25.

A Time of Faithfulness

Monday

. . . be discerned. Talec, *Jesus*, 105.

Tuesday

. . . the day. Evelyn Underhill, *The Fruits of the Spirit*, Treasures from the Spiritual Classics (Wilton, CT: Morehouse Publishing, 1982), 28–29.

Wednesday

. . . given us. Temple, *Christian Faith and Life*, 48–49.

Thursday

. . . and initiative. Evelyn Underhill, *Abba*, Treasures from the Spiritual Classics (Wilton, CT: Morehouse Publishing, 1982), 54.

Friday

. . . whole eternity. Jeremy Taylor, *The Rule and Exercises of Holy Living and the Rule and Exercises of Holy Dying*, Treasures from the Spiritual Classics (Wilton, CT: Morehouse Publishing, 1982), 38–39.

Saturday

. . . exact account. Dom Lorenzo Scupoli, *The Spiritual Combat*, trans. Thomas Barns (London: Methuen & Co., 1909), 149–50.

A Time of Thankfulness

Monday

. . . for you. de Caussade, *Spiritual Letters*, 53.

Tuesday

. . . great things. Pelletier, *Queen of Peace*, 220 (3 October 1985).

Wednesday

. . . those gleams. Andrew, *Life and Letters*, 7–8.

Thursday

. . . promptly respond. Jean Hersey, *The Touch of the Earth* (New York: Seabury Press, 1981), 41.

. . . of joy. Taylor, *Rule and Exercises*, 9.

Friday

. . . is immense! Paul Claudel, *L'annonce faite à Marie*, trans. Molly McConnell, (Paris: Gallimard, 1940), 216.

Saturday

. . . fatherly care. de Caussade, *Spiritual Letters*, 87.

A Time for Change

Monday

. . . in heaven. In Hans Urs von Balthasar, *First Glance at Adrienne von Speyr*, trans. Antje Lawry and Sr. Sergia Englund, O.C.D. (San Francisco: Ignatius Press, 1981), 178.

Tuesday

. . . to God. Underhill, *Light of Christ*, 51–53.

Wednesday

. . . up yet.! White, *Vermont Diary*, 17.

. . . blessed one." Byzantine divine office, in Berselli and Gharib, *Sing the Joys of Mary*, 39, hymn 14.

Thursday

. . . Holy Spirit. Thomas à Kempis, *Christ for All Seasons*, 75.

Friday

. . . holy name. Thomas à Kempis, *Christ for All Seasons*, 35.

. . . transfigures Him. Andrew, *Life and Letters*, 35.

Holy Saturday

. . . Abraham's bosom." Thomas à Kempis, *Christ for All Seasons*, ed. Peter Toon (London: Marshall Morgan and Scott, Marshall Pickering, 1989), 78.

. . . were bound." Thomas à Kempis, *Christ for All Seasons*, 78.

Easter Is Here

Easter

. . . new calves. See Bernard Clayton, Jr., *Complete Book of Breads* (New York: Simon and Schuster, 1987), 345.

Seasonal Recipes

Simnel Cake

Simnel Cake. Mary V. Reilly and Margaret K. Wetterer, *From Thy Bounty* (Wilton, CT: Morehouse Publishing, 1982) 33.

Kulich

Kulich. Reilly and Wetterer, *From Thy Bounty*, 29.

Saints' Days

9 March, Saint Gregory, Bishop of Nyssa

. . .Holy Virgin. Costante Berselli and Georges Gharib, eds., *Sing the Joys of Mary* (Wilton, CT: Morehouse Publishing, 1982) 33, hymn 8.

17 March, Saint Patrick

. . . and stranger. St. Patrick, translated by Cecil Frances Alexander (1818–95), *The Hymnal 1982* (New York: Church Pension Fund, 1985), hymn 370.